50
COMMUNITY
BUILDING
GAMES

VOL 1

DAVID PARIS

ISBN: 9798794922127

CONTENTS

50 COMMUNITY BUILDING GAMES VOL 1 I

CONTENTS V

ACKNOWLEDGEMENTS VII

INTRODUCTION 1

FAQ 2

SECTION 1: ICEBREAKERS 5
   Move Your Butt If...6
   Two Truths and a Lie 7
   Concentric Circles 8
   Opening Check-In 10
   Story Behind Your Name..11

SECTION 2: ENERGIZERS 13
   Zip! Zap! Zop! 14
   Whoosh Ball 16
   Movement Magic 18

SECTION 3: FUN..21
   Carnival Games 22
   Four Corners 24
   Jenga...25
   Jigsaw Puzzle...27
   Juggling Scarves 28
   Loaded Questions..31
   Mirrors 33
   Sounds of the Universe 34
   What Changed? 35
   Barnyard 36

SECTION 4: GROUP CHALLENGES..39
   Group Juggling 40
   Group Knot 42
   Keep It Alive..43
   Maze 45
   Reversal 47
   Ball Toss 49

Caterpillar Walk..50

Silent Line-Up...52

Tower...54

What is the Question?...55

SECTION 5: GYM OR OUTDOOR GAMES **57**

Blob Tag...58

Capture the Flag 59

Go 61

"It" Tag 62

Trust Walk 63

SECTION 6: COMMUNICATION **65**

Back to Back Drawings..66

Blah Blah Blah 67

Creator, Sculptor, and Clay..68

Paper Clip Chain 69

SECTION 7: FEELINGS **71**

Feelings Charades..72

Noticing Your Feelings..73

Emotion Motion 75

SECTION 8: DIALOGUE **77**

Apples to Apples Debates..78

Silly Debate 80

Where Do You Stand?...81

Fishbowl 83

SECTION 9: ACADEMIC REVIEW **85**

Kaboom..86

Guess Who..87

Flash Card Finish 89

SECTION 10: ENDINGS **91**

Shout Outs 92

Riddles, Brain Teasers, and Detective Stories..93

Liked, Learned, and/or Looking Forward To...94

ABOUT THE AUTHOR...95

ACKNOWLEDGEMENTS

Thank you, *Alternatives to Violence Program*, for permission to use your vast collection of games from your basic training manual. Thank you, *American Youth Circus Association*, for permission to use games from your book "Circus Games." Thank you, Erin McCready, the director of *Brooklyn Youth Theater Company*, for introducing me to theater games and bringing a spark to my classrooms for over a decade. Thank you *Outward Bound* for your training on how to bring experiential education to the classroom. And thank you *Restorative Justice Initiative* for your training and leadership in this work.

I am grateful to my principal Ailene Mitchell who allowed me to be one of the first social emotional teachers in the country and is a champion of innovative curriculum. I am indebted to *Ramapo for Children* for their wisdom, guidance, and commitment to the lives of children. Thank you, Zoë Klein, for your feedback and your artful editing which has transformed all my books. And most of all, I am thankful to the thousands of students who have shown me what is possible when we bring the power of games and play back into the classroom.

INTRODUCTION

Games transform classrooms. Ice breakers melt isolation and social anxiety. Energizers awaken dormant minds and bodies. Fun activities create engagement and cohesion. Group challenges spur leadership, collaboration, and belonging. The best games bring out the best in students to build community in the classroom. This book contains fifty of those best games.

The book is written for teachers, by a teacher, with clarity, brevity, and effectiveness in mind. Whether you choose to use a few lessons to brighten up your classroom on a slow day, or utilize the entire book in a comprehensive curriculum, you will see instant energetic change every time you facilitate a game.

The book is divided into 10 sections and are categorized by genre. Each game has at least one variation so that they can be played multiple times and always be a little bit different. There are questions for reflections to process what happened in the game and to extend the learning experiences. There are also Social Emotional Learning standards, created by CASEL.org, to help guide which games to use for your class based on what they need. And finally, there are teacher notes for troubleshooting situations before they even happen.

The selection process for these games was based on 30 years of experimenting on what works and what doesn't in the classroom. The most popular games received the highest star rating. Only games that received at least 3 stars were included.

50 Community Building Games Vol. 1 is an opportunity to bring play back into the classroom, foster connection, and elevate learning. A rich experience of inspiration, creativity, and vitality awaits you and your classroom. Enjoy, venture, and play. Let the games begin!

FAQ

Q: Do I need special training to lead these games?

A: The best training is practice. You will get better each time you try leading these games. Any attempt you make in the direction of community building will be appreciated by your students, no matter what you do.

Q: Can I modify any of the rules?

A: Yes. Modify any rules for safety and the particular needs of a student and class.

Q: How often should I use community building games?

A: I suggest teaching at least one game a week, but energizers can be used more often.

Q: Do I need to have students reflect on the experience?

A: Reflections are crucial to extract the full value of the activity. When students think about their experience, it offers them an opportunity to integrate what happened during the games and possibly extend the lessons to other parts of their lives.

Q: How long should the reflections be?

A: No longer than 5 minutes. I use Outward Bound's three questions for reflection:
- What happened? (Share their experience)
- So what? (Articulate why this was meaningful to them)
- Now what? (How to apply the lesson to other parts of their life)

Q: What if a student is reluctant to participate?

A: I make participation mandatory and treat it no differently than any other part of the curriculum. When possible, I find a different role for a student, like being a judge in a game.

Q: Should students be graded?

A: It depends. For some classrooms, individual grades are antithetical to community building. In other classrooms, grades create accountability, rewards participation, and provides qualitative feedback. In my experience, I found that grades help students engage and take the activities seriously. When time is limited, I have students grade themselves on a scale of 1-4. If time allows, I ask students to write about their experience.

Q: How important are demonstrations?

A: Essential! No matter how well you explain the directions, many students will not understand what to do until they see it. A demonstration with a small group of volunteers always makes the games run more smoothly.

Q: What do I do while students play the games?

A: Students love to be recognized for what they do well. Highlight their creativity and kindness either individually or with the class. By doing so, you will strengthen your connection to your students and reinforce positive behaviors.

Q: Do you suggest journal books devoted to community building games?

A: I have tried this for a couple of years, but the logistics don't work. Journals do have the advantage of keeping all their reflections in one place, but the distribution and collection take up too much time. I have found it's best to have students write their reflection on a loose-leaf sheet of paper or index card and collect these reflections at the end of class.

SECTION 1: ICEBREAKERS

 Great for getting to know each other

 Builds trust in groups

 Gets students talking and listening

 Perfect for the start of the school year

MOVE YOUR BUTT IF...

About: A more active version of "Stand up if..."
Game Type: Icebreaker
SEL Standards: Relationship Skills
Time: 10 mins

Instructions:

1) Have just enough seats in a circle for everyone but one volunteer who agrees to stand in the middle.
2) The volunteer says, "Move your butt if..." and states something physical like, "Move your butt if you are wearing something blue."
3) If a student who is sitting down is wearing blue, they must get up and find another seat anywhere within the circle, except the seat to their immediate left and right.
4) Tell students to move quickly, but also with safety in mind.
5) The student who remains standing without a seat announces the next statement: "Move your butt if..."
6) After a few rounds of physical criteria, introduce statements of...
    a. Preferences such as, "Move your butt if you like ice cream." or
    b. Experiences such as "Move your butt if you have been on a roller coaster."

Variations:

- Tell students to prepare statements about topics they are curious to know about others in the group or what they may have experienced.
- You can play this game without frenetic energy by changing the instruction to 'Stand up if...'

Reflections:

- What was it like to share a commonality with someone else?
- What was it like to be different from the group?

TWO TRUTHS AND A LIE

About:	It's okay to lie, but just once
Type of Game:	Ice Breaker
SEL Standard:	Relationship Skills
Time:	10 mins

Instructions:

1) Divide the class into groups of 4-6 students.
2) Ask one student from each group to share three statements about themselves. Two of the statements should be true, and one should be a lie.
3) Explain that the lies should be based on breaking an expectation or an assumption you think people have of you, rather than changing a simple detail.
4) Have the other students each guess which statement is a lie.
5) The first student then reveals which statement is actually a lie.
6) Rotate roles so that everyone in the group gets at least one chance to share two truths and a lie.

Variations:

- Have students come to consensus about which statements were true and which statements were false before the speaker reveals the answer.
- Do the activity as a class.

Reflections:

- How could you tell what was true and what was a lie?
- What did you think about when you created your own lie?

CONCENTRIC CIRCLES

⭐ ⭐ ⭐ ⭐ ☆

About: Quick conversations for listening and sharing
Type of Game: Ice Breaker
SEL Standard: Relationship Skills
Time: 20 - 30 mins

Instructions:

1) Divide the group in half.
2) Have the group form two circles:
   a. Group A is on the outside and
   b. Group B is on the inside.
3) Have the two groups face each other.
4) Tell Group A that they will be the "talkers" and Group B will be the "listeners."
5) In 30 seconds, ask Group A to share an answer to a prompt.
6) Group B will just listen and ask questions if there is time.
7) After 30 seconds, have Group B answer the prompt and have Group A listen.
8) Have Group A stand up and rotate one seat clockwise.
9) Repeat.

Sample Questions:

1) If you could travel back anywhere in time, when and where would you go and why?
2) If you could have any superpower that would be used for good, what superpower would you choose? How would you use it?
3) What rules are fair and what rules are unfair?
4) What would you do if you found a wallet on the sidewalk?
5) What's the best job in the world? What's the worst?

Variations:

- After students share, they can share their answer with the whole class.
- Students can also share their partner's answers with the class.
- You can alternate which group gets up and rotates. If group A rotates clockwise after the first share, group B can rotate counterclockwise after the second share.

Reflections:

- What was it like to communicate with many students for a small amount of time?
- What was the benefit of this format, and what was challenging?

Teacher Notes:

- This activity can be used throughout the year with academic content and for test preparation.
- If there is not enough space for an inner and outer circle, you can have students sit on the outside edges of the classroom. Then have the students count off "one" and "two" until everyone has a number. Tell the "ones" to turn to their left and the "twos" to turn to their right. After the "ones" and "twos" share and listen, the ones stand up and rotate clockwise.

OPENING CHECK-IN

About: An opportunity for everyone to be heard
Type of Game: Ice Breaker
SEL Standard: Social Awareness / Relationship Skills
Time: 5 - 15 mins

Instructions:

1) Have students share how they are feeling and if there is anything they want to share with the class.

2) Ask students to share a Rose, a Thorn, or a Bud. Students can choose a Rose if something is beautiful and blooming in their life. Students can also share a Thorn if they are facing something challenging or painful. Students can share a Bud, which is something hopeful or exciting that they are looking forward to.

3) Share a famous quote, and have students share what it means to them.

4) Share a poem and have each student read a word or line that is significant or interesting to them.

Teacher Notes:

- Opening check-in takes time to get deep into your students' thoughts. After many iterations, students will share deeper experiences, will have profound questions, and be inspired to share their own experience based on what they heard from others. Encourage this participation. It will lead to meaningful moments.

- When students realize that you are facilitating discussions and not playing a traditional teacher role, more voices will emerge. It is not uncommon for an opening circle to encompass the whole period when you allow topics to emerge that students value.

STORY BEHIND YOUR NAME

About:	This is how you can remember names
Type of Game:	Ice Breaker
SEL Standard:	Relationship Skills
Time:	15 - 20 mins

Instructions:

1) Ask students to share a story about their name. Some ways to do this are:
   a. Students can share who they are named after.
   b. Students can share a story about how their parents came up with their name.
   c. Students can share whether their name has personal meaning to them.
   d. Students can share a story about the tone a parent uses with their name when they are upset with them.

Variations:

- Invite students to share the story of their last names.
- Invite students to share the story of their nicknames.
- After sharing, students can draw their name on a postcard and write their story on it.

Reflections:

- What did you feel when you shared your story?
- What was it like to hear someone else's story?

SECTION 2: ENERGIZERS

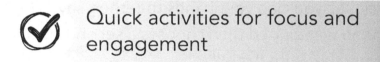 Quick activities for focus and engagement

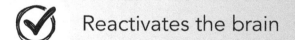 Reactivates the brain

Fulfills students need to move

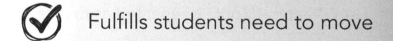 Redirects excess energy

ZIP! ZAP! ZOP!

About:	Wake up time!!!
Type of Game:	Energizer
SEL Standard:	Self-Management
Time:	5- 10 mins

Instructions:

1) Everyone stands in a circle.
2) Start the game by clapping your hands once in the direction towards a student in the circle. As you clap your hands together, say "Zip!"
3) The first student who was zipped then chooses a second student to clap towards while saying the word "Zap!"
4) The student who was zapped then chooses another student to clap towards and says "Zop!"
5) The student who was zopped then chooses another student to clap towards and repeats the pattern as they say, "Zip!"
6) The sequence of "Zip!", "Zap!", "Zop!" is repeated as fast as possible in the group.
7) Anytime there is a word spoken out of sequence, the game starts again.
8) Once students are comfortable with the rules of the game, introduce "Boing!"
9) Students may reject a "Zip!", "Zap!", or "Zop!" by saying "Boing!" as they bob their head.
10) If a student does this, the student that passed the "Zip!", "Zap!", "Zop!" must choose another student to "Zip!", "Zap!", or "Zop!"

Variations:

- This game can be done as an elimination game, with one or multiple winners. This game can also be a speed challenge for the group without anyone being eliminated.

14

- Use high level vocabulary words, scientific concepts, lines for a play, or historical dates and events instead of "Zip!", "Zap!", or "Zop!"

Reflections:

- What strategy did you use to stay focused?
- How does resilience play a role in this activity?

WHOOSH BALL

About: All time great energizer
Type of Game: Energizer
SEL Standard: Self-Management
Time: 5 - 10 mins

Instructions:

1) Arrange students in a large circle either sitting or standing.
2) Start by holding an imaginary ball between your two hands.
3) Pass the ball in one direction around the entire circle.
4) Every time someone passes the ball, have them say "Whoosh."
5) Let everyone have a turn receiving the ball and passing it with their hands to the next person.
6) When the ball comes back to you, hold your palms up to block the pass, and say, "Whoa!"
7) Explain that anyone can block a pass by saying "Whoa" while holding their hands in front of them to block the pass.
8) If the ball is blocked, the ball reverses direction.
9) After the class is comfortable with these rules, add the Zap. Zap is a clap that is directed to another student across the circle.
10) Explain that when you send a Zap, the student who receives the ball has the option to whoosh to the right or the left, or Zap across the circle again to a different person.

Variations:

- Add the "Boing," the recipient of the ball places the palms of their hands together over their head and starts shaking all over. Whenever someone "Boings," everyone in the circle does the same thing (or any predetermined silly movement).

- Add the "Freak Out." The Freak Out means everyone must change places within the circle.
- Play the game with elimination, anytime someone makes a mistake.

Reflections:

- How did you stay alert?
- What was your favorite word and why?

Teacher Note:

- Sometimes, a "Whoa" is followed by another "Whoa" and can go back and forth for some time. Usually, one of the students will break the back-and-forth pattern, but if they don't, it's worth intervening at some point.

MOVEMENT MAGIC

About:	An opportunity to move a little bit and review academic content
Type of Game:	Energizer
SEL Standard:	Self-Management
Time:	5 mins

Instructions:

1) Lead students through a series of stretches.

2) Call out different adverbs to describe the quality of the movement. For example:

   a. Stretch your arms over your head *blissfully*

   b. Circle your head *solemnly*

   c. Reach for your toes *gracefully*

   d. Twist *inquisitively*

3) Repeat the same set of stretches and movements, but this time, call out academic concepts that they can interpret through their stretches. For example:

   a. Stretch your arms over head forming an *acute angle.*

   b. Circle your head demonstrating the movement within a *cell membrane.*

   c. Twist like you're tossing crates of tea off the docks for *the Boston Tea Party.*

Variations:

- Have students lead the movement for the class.
- Use music to accompany the interpretive stretching.

Reflections:

- How did you decide what movement to use?
- What interesting movements did you see other people use?

Teacher Notes:

- This game works best when you model it energetically and enthusiastically.
- Encourage students to move in anyway that works for them.
- Anytime you see a student move in an interesting way, bring positive attention to their movement, and have everyone copy it.

SECTION 3: FUN

✔ Captivating games that build community and feelings of belonging

✔ Opportunities to practice social emotional learning

✔ Creates shared experiences of joy, challenge, and laughter

✔ Teaches applicable lessons for life

CARNIVAL GAMES

⭐ ⭐ ⭐ ⭐ ⭐

About: Grand opportunity to practice resilience and
                    positive habits of mind
Type of Game: Fun
SEL Standard: Self-Management / Responsible Decision-Making
Time: 30 - 35 mins

Supplies:

- (5) small plastic water bottle filled one third of the way full
- (5) feathers
- carnival games: ring toss, sticky ball darts, bean bag throw

Instructions:

1) Divide the class into 5 groups.
2) Explain that each group will have 5 minutes at each station.
3) Explain how to do each of the 5 stations:
    - feather balancing
    - water bottle challenge
    - ring toss
    - sticky ball darts
    - bean bag throw
4) Note that:
    a. both the feather balance and the water bottle challenge stations will allow all students in a group to play at once.
    b. The other stations require students to take turns.

Variations:

- Choose one game and try to perfect the skill for longer periods of time.
- Tally the success at each station and have the groups compete against each other.

Reflections:

- How did you overcome adversity or lack of success?
- What did you learn that you can bring to other challenges in your life?

Teacher Notes:

- Sometimes there is only time for doing half of the games. When this happens, tell the students that you will complete the rotation the next time you see them.
- I like to use ostrich feathers, which are relatively easy to balance.

FOUR CORNERS

About:	High interest game involving randomness
Type of Game:	Fun
SEL Standard:	Self-Awareness
Time:	15 - 20 mins

Instructions:

1) One student is chosen to be The Pointer. They must stand in the middle of the room, close their eyes, and count to ten.
2) During this time, the rest of the students go to any of the four corners of the room quietly.
3) When The Pointer finishes counting, they spin at least three times. Then they randomly stop, point, and open their eyes.
4) All students that are in the corner closest to where the pointer is pointing are now eliminated.
5) Repeat until there is one student left.

Variation:

- You can have students go to the corners of the room based on how strongly they feel about a prompt you read on a scale of 1-4.

Reflections:
- How do you deal with random elimination, not based on your skill or effort?
- Where in life do we deal with random obstacles or challenges?

JENGA

About:	The greatest combination of resilience games ever created
Type of Game:	Fun
SEL Standard:	Self-Management / Responsible Decision-Making
Time:	30 - 40 mins

Supplies:

- (6) boxes of Jenga

Instructions:

1) Divide the students into 6 groups.
2) Explain the rules for Jenga.
3) Explain that their task is to notice how they deal with the structure falling apart:
    a. Do they tell themselves that mistakes happen?
    b. Do they allow themselves to learn from mistakes?
    c. How do they handle the task emotionally?
    d. What is there to learn about bouncing back when things fall apart?

Variations:

- Make each round a speed round
- Have groups compete against each other for the title of the most interesting structure

Reflections:

- What did you learn about resilience?
- How did you react when your structure collapsed? How was your reaction similar or different to other times in your life when things fell apart?

Teacher Notes:

- Retaining game pieces is not easy. Have a student check play areas for missing pieces or make one student for each group accountable for returning all the game pieces.
- Some students like to play dominoes with the Jenga pieces, usually after 5 to 10 minutes.

JIGSAW PUZZLE

About: Teamwork always wins
Type of Game: Fun
SEL Standard: Relationship Skills
Time: 30 -40 mins

Supplies:

- (6) 100 Piece jigsaw games

Instructions:

1) Divide students into 6 groups.
2) Give students 20 minutes to complete the puzzle.

Variations:

- Use a 200-piece jigsaw puzzle.
- Have students use one hand only.

Reflections:
- How did your group work as a team?
- What strategy did you use?

Teacher Notes:

- I recommend having students count the pieces before returning them to the box.
- It is also useful to mark the back of each piece with different colors coordinated to its corresponding puzzle box. This way, if a piece is found, you know which box to return it to.

JUGGLING SCARVES

⭐ ⭐ ⭐ ⭐ ⭐

About: Everyone can do it
Type of Game: Fun
SEL Standard: Self-Awareness / Self Management / Relationship Skills
Time: 15 - 30 mins

Supplies:

- (4) dozen juggling scarves
- (1) bag for storing the scarves

Instructions:

1) Place the juggling scarves in a bag.

2) Explain that many students new to juggling often start with juggling scarves because they float a long time in the air.

3) Divide the class into 2, group A and group B.

4) Match one student from group A with one student from group B.

5) Tell Student A that they will practice for 2 minutes while Student B offers support and coaching. Then the students will switch roles.

6) Have Group A take one scarf out of the bag and hold it.

7) Demonstrate different tossing patterns with ONE scarf:

   a. Throw with your right hand, catch with your right hand.

   b. Throw with your left hand, catch with your left hand.

   c. Throw diagonally with your right hand, catch with your left hand

   d. Throw diagonally with your left hand, catch with your right hand.

   e. Throw behind the back with your left hand, catch with your right hand.

    f.   Throw behind the back with your right hand, catch with your left hand.

    g.   Let students know they can be creative to invent any other pattern with one scarf.

8) After both groups practice juggling, reflect on the experience.

9) Have Group A take a second scarf out of the bag.

10) Demonstrate tossing patterns with TWO scarves:

    a.   Start with the right hand, toss two scarves, and only catch with the right hand.

    b.   Start with the left hand, toss two scarves, and only catch with the left hand.

    c.   Start with one scarf in the right hand and one scarf in the left hand. Toss both in the air and then catch with the same hand.

    d.   Start with one scarf in the right hand and one scarf in the left hand again, but this time, toss diagonally and catch with the other hand, one at a time.

    e.   Toss in a circular motion.

    f.   Give the option to add creative flourishes.

11) Give 4 minutes each to practice 2 scarves.

12) Demonstrate THREE scarves:

    a.   Start with a circular pattern.

    b.   Attempt a diagonal tossing pattern.

13) Give 4 minutes each to practice 3 scarves.

Variations:

- Increase the time.
- Have students use one hand.
- Have students repeat the same chronological order but pass the scarves to each other in pairs or larger groups.
- Use real juggling balls.

Reflections:

- How did you deal with the challenge of focusing on different objects at the same time?
- What was it like to have a coach?

Teacher Notes:

- It's possible to do without the coaches. But it tends to be too chaotic to have everyone playing at the same time.
- You can show an instructional juggling scarves video from Youtube.

LOADED QUESTIONS

⭐ ⭐ ⭐ ⭐ ⭐

About:	Great guessing game
Type of Game:	Fun
SEL Standard:	Relationship Skills / Responsible Decision Making
Time:	20 mins

Supplies:

- (5 packs) "Loaded Questions Junior"
- (5-6) sheets of paper of the same size and color

Instructions:

1) Divide the class into groups of 5-6 students.
2) Have students use their paper to record their answers with their names on top.
3) The paper should all be the same size and color, so the answers can remain anonymous.
4) The reader chooses a question from the card, and everyone writes their answer down.
5) The reader collects the answers, shuffles the papers, and reads the answers one by one.
6) Apart from the reader, have students guess who wrote the answer.
7) The student who actually wrote the answer should point to someone else confidently, to throw off suspicion.
8) After everyone points to someone, the reader reveals who actually wrote the answer.
9) This process continues until all the answers are read.
10) The winner is the student who has the most correct guesses after all answers are read.
11) Rotate the readers so everyone has a chance.

Variation:

- Play as a class.

Reflections:

- What did you learn about your classmates?
- What surprised you?

Teacher Notes:

- These instructions are adapted for creating the most student participation, but all rules are adaptable to what works best in your classroom.
- This is a good game to play at the beginning of the year to help students get to know each other better.

MIRRORS

★ ★ ★ ★ ★

About: Perfect for energy, movement, and play
Type of Game: Fun
SEL Standard: Social Awareness / Relationship Skills
Time: 10 mins

Instructions:

1) Students are divided into pairs and face each other. One person is the Mover. The other person is the Mirror.
2) The Mover moves slowly while the Mirror copies everything the Mover does.
3) Tell the students to switch roles after 1 minute.

Variations:

- Work in groups with one Mover and multiple Mirrors.
- Have students exchange roles on their own.
- Have the student in the role of Mirror interpret the movement, instead of simply mirroring the movement.
- Have the student in the role of Mirror do the opposite of the Mover.
- Have the Mover just move their hands, or one other isolated body part, while the Mirror translates what they see into bigger movements.
- Have the Mover stand in front of the class while everyone else is in the role of multiple mirrors.

Reflections:

- What did you do to stay focused?
- How does empathy play a role in this activity?

SOUNDS OF THE UNIVERSE

★ ★ ★ ★ ★

About:	The group helps a lost student find their destination
Type of Game:	Fun
SEL Standard:	Relationship Skills
Time:	10 mins

Instructions:

1) Ask for one volunteer to step out of the room.
2) Ask someone else to choose a spot in the room for the volunteer to find.
3) Ask for the volunteer to return to the room.
4) As the student enters the room, have students indicate how close or far the volunteer is to the spot by the intensity of their clap of hands or thighs.
5) If the volunteer goes away from the spot, lessen the intensity.
6) If the volunteer goes towards the spot, increase the intensity.
7) Celebrate when the volunteer hits the spot.
8) Repeat!

Variations:

- Have two volunteers and divide the rest of the class into two groups. These groups can each be assigned a volunteer and compete over who can find the spot the fastest.
- Use facial expressions to guide volunteers, without any sound.
- In addition to finding the spot, have them do a specific and easy-to-do task.

Reflections:

- What did it feel like to collectively help a classmate?
- What did it feel like to get support from the entire class?

WHAT CHANGED?

★ ★ ★ ★ ★

About:	A great game to test our observation skills
Type of Game:	Fun
SEL Standard:	Relationship Skills
Time:	10 - 15 mins

Instructions:

1) Divide the class into pairs.
2) Have students study the appearance of their partner for thirty seconds.
3) Have the students turn back-to-back and change three things about their appearance in thirty seconds. For example:
   a. untie a shoe
   b. open a button
   c. change hair
4) Partners turn back to face each other and guess what the three changes were.
5) Find a new partner.

Variation:

- Have one student leave the room and change three things about the room's appearance.

Reflections:

- Were you good at noticing details?
- How did the class decide what things to change within the classroom?

BARNYARD

About:	Who wants to cluck like a chicken and moo like a cow?
Type of Game:	Fun
SEL Standard:	Relationship Skills
Time:	10 - 15 mins

Supplies:

- (30) slips of paper
- (1) Plastic or canvas bag

Instructions:

1) Write the names of 5-6 different types of barnyard animals (chickens, goats, ducks, cows, pigs, sheep, rabbits, cats, dogs) on 30 slips of paper, and place them in a bag.
2) Have students each take one slip of paper from the bag and read it to themselves without showing anyone.
3) Tell students to find the other students who have the same barnyard animal by making sounds and movements that would help others know what animal they have.
4) At the end of 5 minutes, have students reveal to each other their animals to make sure they are in the right group.

Variations:

- This game can also be played by making barnyard animal movements and not sounds.
- Use academic vocabulary to review a lesson. For example, you could replace barnyard animals with geometric shapes, weather patterns, characters from a book, or historical figures.

Reflections:

- What movements did you make to demonstrate your barnyard animal?
- What did it feel like to find your group?

SECTION 4:
GROUP CHALLENGES

✓ Promotes critical thinking and problem solving

✓ Develops leadership, collaboration, and decision making

✓ Improves feelings of cohesion and purpose

✓ Offers powerful moments for both self and group reflection

GROUP JUGGLING

About:	Great for fun, positive feedback, and talking about support
Type of Game:	Group Challenge
SEL Standard:	Self-Management / Social Awareness / Relationship Skills
Time:	10-20 mins

Supplies:

- (20) Tennis balls or Koosh balls

Instructions:

1) Divide students into groups of 7-10 students and have them stand in a circle.
2) Explain that they will be juggling one or more tennis balls as a group.
3) Choose someone who will start the group juggle. That student will pass one ball underhanded to another student anywhere in the circle.
4) The student who receives the ball will then pass the ball to someone different in the circle.
5) Passes are always thrown to someone who has not had a ball tossed to them yet.
6) This continues until everyone gets a chance to have a ball tossed to them.
   a. When possible, students should not pass the ball to someone next to them.
   b. If the ball drops, the group repeats the same passing pattern that was established when the first student tossed the ball to the second student.
7) When the ball reaches the last person, that student will then toss the ball back to the first student.
8) Once everyone has touched the ball, the passing pattern has been established. Tell the class they will now repeat the established pattern but ask them to try to do it a little faster.

9) After the group seems confident with this faster pattern, tell the group they can now graduate to tossing two balls, one at a time. NOTE:
   a. They can keep adding balls into the group juggle every time they successfully toss the balls to everyone without having them touch the ground.
   b. There is almost no limit to the number of balls that can be added.

Variations:

- Groups can add a verbal challenge such as saying the student's name when passing them the ball.
- Groups can reverse the passing pattern after they complete their first passing pattern.
- The group can simultaneously toss the original passing pattern AND the reverse pattern using two balls.
- The circle can move clockwise or counterclockwise as students pass the ball.

Reflections:

- What can this activity teach us about how to support each other as a group?
- How can you change what you do in an activity to help someone else?

Teacher Notes:
- It is important to emphasize underhand tosses. If not, someone will mistake the activity for a professional baseball game.
- Demonstrate with a small group and show that when mistakes happen, the group can support each other.
- This is a great activity to check in midway and celebrate any positive displays of support. This support might mean giving information on how to catch, or how to toss a ball so someone can catch it more easily.

GROUP KNOT

★ ★ ★ ★ ★

About: What seems impossible is possible
Type of Game: Group Challenge
SEL Standard: Self-Management / Social Awareness / Relationship Skills
Time: 10-20 mins

Instructions:

1) Divide the students into groups of 7-9 students and have them stand in a circle shoulder to shoulder.
2) Each person puts their hands into the center of the circle.
3) Have students grab a hand from two different people. They cannot choose anyone directly next to them in the circle.
4) The challenge is to become "untangled" without letting go.
5) The group should end up in a large circle, however, sometimes two circles can form.

Variation:

- Have groups compete against each other.

Reflections:

- What role did leadership play in this activity?
- What feelings emerged with this challenge?

Teacher Notes:

- When students get stuck, allow them to rotate their hands, but they cannot let go.
- Sometimes two circles form at the end. That is okay.

KEEP IT ALIVE

★ ★ ★ ★ ★

About: Another classic game with a group twist
Type of Game: Group Challenge
SEL Standard: Self-Management / Social Awareness / Relationship Skills
Time: 15-20 mins

Supplies:

- (12) Beach Balls or balloons

Instructions:

1) Divide students into groups of 6-8 students.
2) Have students link elbows or hands.
3) Tell students that they will try to keep the ball or balloon off the ground as they bump it into the air at least 20 times.
4) If the ball or balloon touches the ground, they must start the count over.
5) If the students separate their connections, they also must start the counting over.
6) They can use any of their arms or their shoulders to toss the ball or balloon, but not their head or legs.
7) Feet must stay in place unless you are outdoors and there is more room to play.

Variations:

- Each student may only hit the ball or balloon once until everyone hits it.
- Each student can move one foot.
- Add multiple balls or balloons.

Reflections:

- What problems did you face and how did you solve them?
- What was it like to have individual ambitions, but limitations based on the group?

Teacher Notes:

- Using the head as a striking point may lead to soccer-style injury. Best to not permit head bumps.
- Balloons are possible substitutions for beach balls, but are not great outdoors, as the wind can be challenging, or they may pop more easily.
- It's possible to facilitate this game with one group at a time in the classroom.

MAZE

⭐ ⭐ ⭐ ⭐ ⭐

About:	Another classic game with a group twist
Type of Game:	Group Challenge
SEL Standard:	Self-Management / Social Awareness / Relationship Skills
Time:	15-20 mins

Supplies:

- Masking tape

Instructions:

1) Make a 4-foot by 4-foot grid with masking tape. If there is a tile floor, mark off a 4-tile by 4-tile grid. The squares should be large enough for two feet to stand inside.
2) Divide students into three groups of 7-10 students.
3) Have students in Group A line up to try to cross the grid within 5 minutes while the other groups watch. To cross the grid successfully, the group must follow a secret walking pattern/combination.
4) Create a secret walking pattern/combination/maze for students to follow that starts on one side and ends on the other side. There are no diagonals and students can not step into the same box twice.
5) Students must learn the secret walking pattern through trial and error.
6) If a student walks into a box that is part of the secret walking pattern you created, say nothing (the silence is part of the drama). They can then proceed to another square.
7) If the box is not correct, make a buzzer sound. They must go to the back of the line within their group, then wait their turn to start again.
8) When one student makes it across the square, the next student in line must successfully repeat the same walking pattern.
9) If any successive student steps into the wrong box, all the students must go back and start again.

10) The game ends when all members of the group make it to the other side, one by one.

11) After Group A finishes, mark the time and the other groups try to cross the grid with a new secret walking pattern.

Variations:

- Allow diagonals.
- Have all students be silent.
- Increase the size of the grid such as 5-feet by 5-feet.
- Allow multiple students in a group onto the grid at the same time.

Reflections:

- How did you feel about the trial-and-error process?
- Were you able to learn from other students' mistakes?

Teacher Notes:

- It's possible to divide the class into two groups, but participation lags when groups are this large.
- When you explain the rules, demonstrate a super easy pattern so the concept will be understood, and can be done quickly.
- Some students who are watching like to see the answer and participate in the buzzing.
- It's important to have students step into one square at a time and determine wheather that step is part of the walking pattern before they step into another square.
- Make each group maze progressively harder since groups that are second or third have an advantage of seeing what worked for the other groups. One way to make the mazes more complicated is to add steps. For example, after stepping sideways, they might have to step backwards.

REVERSAL

★ ★ ★ ★ ★

About:	When lining up is not enough
Type of Game:	Group Challenge
SEL Standard:	Self-Management / Social Awareness / Relationship Skills
Time:	15 mins

Supplies:

- Masking tape

Instructions:

1) Divide students into three groups.
2) Mark off a row of tiles or make a 6-inch by 10-foot rectangle using masking tape.
3) Have one group step on that row of tiles or line of masking tape.
4) Explain that their challenge is to reverse the order of the group in the line without stepping outside the row of tiles or rectangle.
5) The group that does it the fastest wins.
6) If anyone steps outside the row of tiles, or off the tape, the whole process starts from the beginning.
7) Each group has 10 minutes to complete this challenge.

Variations:

- Have groups start one at a time and have bystanders watch silently.
- Increase group size.

Reflections:

- How did the group consider ideas?
- Did it seem hopeless?

Teacher Notes:

- Sometimes students will use leaning on furniture as a strategy. Others will use their hands on the floor. It's a choice whether to allow this.
- Hopping over each other should not be allowed for safety. Carrying each other could work and should be assessed on an individual basis. It is best when everyone can be respectful of each other's bodies.
- If you have multiple groups doing the group challenge at the same time, you will need an extra pair of eyes to judge whether anyone stepped off the line or row of tiles. There are usually many eager volunteers for this role.

BALL TOSS

★ ★ ★ ★ ☆

About:	How many balls can your group toss at the same time?
Type of Game:	Group Challenge
SEL Standard:	Self-Management / Social Awareness / Relationship Skills
Time:	10-20 mins

Supplies:

- (20) Tennis balls or Koosh balls

Instructions:

1) Divide students into groups of 6-8 students.
2) Ask one player to throw a ball to another player.
3) If the ball is not caught by the other player, and instead falls to the ground, have the group try again.
4) If the catch is successful, have the group add another ball.
5) With each successful toss and catch, add another ball.
6) With multiple balls, all throws must happen simultaneously.

Reflections:

- What was challenging with the addition of the new balls?
- What strategies did you use for success?

CATERPILLAR WALK

⭐ ⭐ ⭐ ⭐ ☆

About: Not as easy as it seems
Type of Game: Group Challenge
SEL Standard: Self-Management / Relationship Skills
Time: 15-25 mins

Supplies:

- (10) 6-inch cardboard squares

Instructions:

1) Divide students into two groups behind a starting line.
2) Establish a finishing line on the other side of the room.
3) Explain that there is a river flowing between the starting and finishing line.
4) Place cardboard squares in between the starting and finishing line as islands.
5) The islands offer both groups equal opportunity with separate pathways to get across the classroom.
6) The challenge is that students must cross in pairs while stepping on the islands *and* while also using the outside of one foot to maintain contact with their partner.
7) If students step anywhere off the islands, everyone in the group must go back to the starting line.
8) If a student's foot gets disconnected as they cross the river, the whole group must start again.
9) The groups will be competing against each other.

Variations:

- Increase the number of students that are linked together from two to three or four.
- Change the space between islands.

Reflections:

- How did you work together as a group?
- How did you balance speed with being careful?

Teacher Note:

- This game is sometimes played with students tying their shoelaces together. This works until students face the difficulty of untying their shoes.

SILENT LINE-UP

★ ★ ★ ★ ☆

About: A fun way to have students make a line
Type of Game: Group Challenge
SEL Standard: Self-Management / Social Awareness / Relationship Skills
Time: 5-10 mins

Instructions:

1) Divide students into two groups of 10-15 students.
2) Explain that this activity is silent.
3) Tell students that they will have 4 minutes to line themselves up by the month and day of their birthday (not including year).

Variations:

- Restrict the techniques they use for success, such as:
  - No mouthing words to each other,
  - No writing,
  - No using fingers to form letters or numbers,
- Have students line up alphabetically using their last name, or their favorite animal.

Reflections:

- What strategies did you use?
- Were you surprised by the results?

Alternative Prompts for Line Up:

- By City/State/Country Born
- By spelling your first name backward
- By whom lives closest to the school (Closest-Furthest Away)
- By the average amount of minutes they are on social media in a day

Teacher Note:

- This game is a great set up for the game titled Reversal.

TOWER

About: Creating community one building block at a time
Type of Game: Group Challenge
SEL Standard: Self-Management / Social Awareness / Relationship Skills
Time: 15-20 mins

Supplies:

- Playing cards
- plastic cups
- copy paper
- anything that is stackable

Instructions:

1) Divide students into groups of 4.
2) Each group has 10 min to create the highest structure possible using the materials you provide.
3) The structure must be intact at the end of 10 minutes.
4) If students use playing cards, make sure they know they are not allowed to bend the cards.
5) Students can't touch any other group's construction.

Variation:

- Add a round 2 with a shorter time limit or new materials.

Reflections:

- How did you generate ideas as a group?
- How did you respond to ideas that didn't work?

WHAT IS THE QUESTION?

★ ★ ★ ☆ ☆

About:	A twist on Jeopardy
Type of Game:	Group Challenge
SEL Standard:	Relationship Skills / Responsible Decision-Making
Time:	10 - 20 mins

Instructions:

1) Divide the class into groups of 4.

2) Explain that instead of asking them a question, you will be giving them an answer.

3) It is their job to determine the question.

4) The task is to come up with as many questions as you can within 2 minutes.

5) Give examples. If the answer is 18, the question can be:

    a. "What's the voting age?" or

    b. "How many eggs are in a dozen and a half?" or

    c. "How many compliments can you give your teacher before they know you want something in return?"

6) Repeat as many times as you like.

Reflections:

- Was it difficult to questions?
- How did you create questions that were out of the box?

Sample Answers:

- Cell phones
- Valentine's Day
- Purple
- Magic wands
- Sea turtles
- Crazy glue
- Lettuce
- Tik Tok

SECTION 5:
GYM OR OUTDOOR GAMES

✓ Provides a new paradigm for success based on cooperation

✓ Inspires strategic thinking

✓ Integrates body and mind

✓ Perfect for field day and recess

BLOB TAG

About:	Second best tag game ever
Type of Game:	Gym / Outdoors
SEL Standard:	Social Management / Relationship Skills / Responsible Decision-Making
Time:	20 mins

Instructions:

1) The game starts with one student who is "It."
2) Whenever that student tags someone else, they link elbows or hands and chase other students.
3) The Blob must stay linked as it grows and chases other students.

Variations:

- Increase the number of Blobs that start each round and have the Blobs compete against each other to capture other students.
- Change movement style from running to shuffling, skipping, or side stepping.

Reflections:

- How did you work as a team to achieve a bigger Blob?
- How does this activity relate to respect?
- When you were not in the Blob, what strategies did you use to elude the Blob?

Teacher Notes:

- Students will sometimes break apart from their Blob to capture students. If this happens, add a rule that if a Blob separates, the Blob must freeze for 30 seconds.
- The first round should be timed and short lived. It gets far more interesting when there are multiple blobs competing against each other.

CAPTURE THE FLAG

About: Endless fun
Type of Game: Gym / Outdoors
SEL Standard: Self-Management / Relationship Skills / Decision-Making
Time: 15-30 mins

Instructions:

1) Divide the class into two teams.

2) Divide the playing field in half. Create sidelines and end lines.

3) Explain that each team will have a territory to attack and defend.

4) Place one flag (can be a stuffed animal, a ball, or even a small flag) in the back of each territory.

5) Designate a holding zone for anyone who gets captured in enemy territory.

6) Explain that the object of the game is to get the flag from the other team's territory and bring it back to your territory.

7) If a student gets tagged by the other team in their territory, they are captured and go to their holding zone.

8) If a student grabs the flag in the other team's territory, and they get tagged on the way back to their team's territory, that student is captured and the flag returns to its original position.

9) You can only be released from a holding zone if someone from their team tags them while they wait in the holding zone. If anyone in the holding zone is tagged, everyone is freed. Players who are freed must immediately go back to their territory and have temporary immunity until they get there.

10) If a student is defending their flag, they must be at least 10 feet away from it, and not hover over their flag.

Variations:

- Assign a spy on each team.
- Divide the class into 4 groups and have a tournament for first, second, third, and last place.

Reflections:

- What strategy did your team use?
- How did you use teamwork?

Teacher Note:

- There are often disputes about whether someone was tagged or not, so it's advisable to have some students be judges.

GO

About: Third best tag game of all time
Type of Game: Gym / Outdoors
SEL Standard: Self-Management / Relationship Skills / Decision-Making
Time: 10 - 15 mins

Instructions:

1) Create a rectangular playing space and designate one volunteer in the middle with the role of "It." Everyone else stands behind a starting line.
2) The "It" student yells "Go," and everyone runs to the other side of the playing field.
3) Runners are only safe if they reach the other ending line.
4) The "It" will tag as many students as they can.
5) Anyone who is tagged also becomes "It" and then attempts to tag other students remaining in the playing space.
6) When all the players are either tagged or behind the finishing line, another round begins.
7) The stating and ending line are reversed.
8) The original student who was "It" announces "Go" again, and anyone who is also "It" will try to tag players as they cross the field.
9) Repeat until there is no one left.

Variations:

- Change movements to skips, hops, shuffles, and more.
- Have students move according to characters in literature or using adverbs.
- Have anyone who gets tagged take a knee. Once the student takes a knee, they can tag other students.

Reflections:

- What strategy did you use?
- What was it like to work as a team?

"IT" TAG

About: Best tag game of all time
Type of Game: Gym / Outdoors
SEL Standard: Self-Management / Relationship Skills / Decision-Making
Time: 10 - 15 mins

Instructions:
1) Every player is "It."
2) Students try to tag other people before being tagged themselves.
3) If tagged, the student takes a knee.
4) If there's a dispute about who tagged who first, have students play rock paper scissors.
5) The last student standing wins.

Variations:
- Change movement styles to shuffling, skipping, or hopping.
- Students who take a knee still can tag someone who is not "out."
- Have a "Revivor" give students who have been tagged new life.
- Give three lives, or one life if a student gets tagged in the back.
- Have students run with bean bags on their heads. If the bean bag drops, they take a knee.
- Narrow boundaries to increase action.

Reflections:
- What strategies did you use?
- How did you bounce back from defeat?
- What did you learn from losing?

Teacher Notes:
- Give a time limit of 30 seconds when there are only a few students left.
- Students figure out to have alliances. Instead of fighting it, it's best to work with it, and make teams.

TRUST WALK

★ ★ ★ ★ ☆

About: A powerful exploration of trust and being trustworthy
Type of Game: Gym / Outdoors
SEL Standard: Self-Management / Relationship Skills / Decision-Making
Time: 15 - 20 mins

Instructions:

1) Divide students into pairs.
2) One student will be "Guided" the other student will be the "Guide".
3) The Guide will stand behind the Guided and place their hands on his or her shoulders.
4) The Guided closes their eyes.
5) The Guide will use their hands to lead the Guided.
6) The Guide can go in any direction, but most importantly, can also stop if there is an obstacle ahead.
7) After one minute, switch roles.

Variations:

- Create trios and quartets, with the person in the back guiding everyone in front of them. All the students in the middle also close their eyes and have their hands on all the shoulders of the person in front of them. Note: communication takes longer to pass from the back to the front of the line.
- Create an obstacle course.
- Have pairs retrieve items.

Reflections:

- What is it like to trust someone else?
- Did you struggle being trustworthy?
- How do we deal with people who break our trust?

SECTION 6: COMMUNICATION

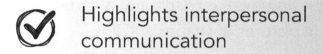 Highlights interpersonal communication

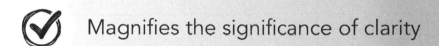 Magnifies the significance of clarity

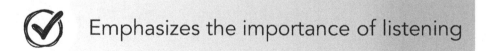 Emphasizes the importance of listening

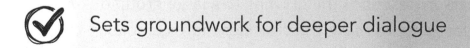 Sets groundwork for deeper dialogue

BACK TO BACK DRAWINGS

⭐ ⭐ ⭐ ⭐ ⭐

About: Brings awareness to the importance of specific language
Type of Game: Communication
SEL Standard: Relationship Skills
Time: 15 - 20 mins

Supplies:
- Blank paper

Instructions:
1) Divide the group into pairs.
2) Have students sit or stand back-to-back.
3) Student A draws a simple picture with at least 2 geometric shapes in 30 sec.
4) So that students are clear that this exercise is not an art competition, give a few samples using simple pictures of shapes and lines.
5) Student A has 2 minutes to describe how to draw their picture. Student B listens, is not allowed to talk, and does their best job to replicate the picture.
6) Compare the pictures.
7) Switch roles and repeat the process.
8) Repeat activity with the same partner or a new partner.

Variations:
- You can give out preset drawings for students to describe.
- One person describes the drawing to a large group of 3-4.
- Add more time to make the drawings more complex.
- Play a second round and allow Student B to ask questions.
- Instead of creating drawings, use blocks, Legos, or craft materials.

Reflections:
- Did your drawings look like what was described?
- What was difficult about describing the image? About listening?
- What did you learn about communication?

BLAH BLAH BLAH

About: A primer for body language and tone
Type of Game: Communication
SEL Standard: Relationship Skills
Time: 10 - 15 mins

Instructions:

1) Divide students into pairs.
2) Assign all students with a character, setting, and conflict. Use examples such as...
   a. Two friends find a wallet on the street. One friend wants to keep it, the other friend wants to find the rightful owner.
   b. A customer is upset with the waiter at a restaurant because the soup is cold.
   c. A parent tries to fix a child's shirt for a photo at home, but the child doesn't want to be bothered.
3) Within those parameters, the two students engage in a conversation using only the word "blah," using tone and nonverbal communication to convey meaning.

Variations:

- Only tell Student A the Who, What, Where. After a "blah" conversation, have Student B guess the Who, What, and Where.
- Try this with three different people.
- Try the same activity without any words, not even using "blah".
- Try the same activity without any movement, just "blah" and tone.

Reflections:

- What were you able and unable to communicate?
- How did your physicality and tone affect comprehension?

CREATOR, SCULPTOR, AND CLAY

⭐⭐⭐⭐☆

About: An illumination of the importance of language
Type of Game: Communication
SEL Standard: Relationship Skills
Time: 15 - 20 mins

Instructions:

1) Divide the class into groups of 3.
2) Each student chooses a role - Creator, Sculptor, or Clay.
3) Explain that everyone will have a chance to do each role.
4) The Creator stands back-to-back with Clay.
5) The Creator creates a shape that they can sustain for 1 minute.
6) The Sculptor tells the Clay how to move so they are in the same position as the Creator.
7) After 1 minute, the Creator turns around and observes the Sculptor's work.
8) Everyone should switch roles and repeat until each person has been in each role.

Variations:

- Increase the difficulty by telling the Creator to move one or more limbs in a consistent pattern.
- You can increase group size to 5 students and have two Creators and two Clays.

Reflections:

- What was different about each role?
- What was challenging?

PAPER CLIP CHAIN

About:	Not as bad as threading a needle, but close
Type of Game:	Communication
SEL Standard:	Relationship Skills
Time:	10 mins

Supplies:

- (3) boxes of paper clips

Instructions:

1) Divide students into pairs.
2) Tell students that they are going to compete against other groups to create the longest chain of paper clips possible. However, Student A will have their eyes closed while Student B will only be allowed to instruct Student A what to do.
3) At the end of 5 minutes, tally the number of paper clips on each pair's chain.
4) Have the students switch roles.
5) Once the competition is over, you can have students compete over disassembling the chains and placing all the paper clips back in the box.

Variations:

- Have both students open their eyes, but each student can only use their non-dominant hand.
- Compete in groups.

Reflections:

- What was difficult to communicate with?
- Was assembling or disassembling the chain harder?

SECTION 7: FEELINGS

- ☑ First steps in an empathy curriculum

- ☑ Promotes self-regulation

- ☑ Cultivates a relationship to a feelings vocabulary

- ☑ Improves understanding of oneself and others

FEELINGS CHARADES

⭐ ⭐ ⭐ ⭐ ⭐

About:	An awesome engaging twist on a traditional game
Type of Game:	Feelings
SEL Standard:	Self-Awareness / Social Awareness
Time:	10 – 15 mins

Supplies:
- (80) index cards. Each card has one feeling word written on it.

Instructions:
1) Divide the class into four groups and have each group form a circle.
2) Place four decks of 20 feeling index cards each within the center of every circle.
3) Ask for a volunteer to go to the middle of the circle.
4) This volunteer will choose one feeling index card. They then will choose a pose that demonstrates that feeling.
5) The students in the circle will guess which emotion the volunteer is expressing.
6) This volunteer may not speak during their pose, but they will need to indicate whether a guess is correct or not.
7) The other students guess the feeling associated with the gesture.
8) Each student goes into the middle of the circle at least once.
9) After 5 minutes, have the groups rotate to a new set of feeling cards.

Variation:
- Have students add a monologue to their pose.

Reflections:
- What nonverbal cues were you able to detect in order to make an empathy guess?
- When and how is this skill useful in life?

NOTICING YOUR FEELINGS

About:	You are always feeling something
Type of Game:	Feelings
SEL Standard:	Self-Awareness / Social Awareness
Time:	15 mins

Supplies:

- Any small item you can put in a student's palm
- Paper and pen/pencil

Instructions:

1) Tell students that this exercise is a training to notice our feelings.

2) Announce to the class: "Everyone is going to get a gift."

3) Tell students to write down whatever they feel at the moment they hear this announcement. Give some examples of potential feelings: excitement, surprise, indifference, nervousness.

4) Tell students that to get the gift, they will have to put their elbows on their thighs and hold their palms out.

5) Ask them, "How do you feel?" and have them write that down.

6) Tell them to close their eyes. Say, "You will now receive your gift, but you have to keep your eyes closed when you receive your gift in your hand."

7) Ask them, "How do you feel?" and have them write that down.

8) Tell them that for the next few feelings, their eyes will be closed, so they don't have to write them down.

9) Once every student has their eyes closed, tell them that it will take one minute to walk around the room and put the gift in everyone's hand. Ask them to notice what they are feeling.

10) Ask students to stay quiet as you walk around. Put one item in the palm of each hand.

11) Tell the students to close their hands and notice the texture of the gift, while noticing what they are feeling.

12) Tell students to open their hands and eyes and notice how they are feeling.

13) Have students turn and talk to their neighbor about what they experienced.

14) Ask students to complete the feelings list.

Variations:

- Change the item.
- Add a list of feelings beforehand.

Reflections:

- Did you feel something at all times? Feeling numb, indifferent, or bored is still a feeling.
- Did you experience your feelings change from moment to moment?

EMOTION MOTION

About: Empathy guesses through body language
Type of Game: Feelings
SEL Standard: Self-Awareness / Social Awareness
Time: 10 – 15 mins

Instructions:

1) Have students form a circle.
2) Have Student A go outside the classroom. While that student is gone, the rest of the group chooses an emotion, such as joy or fear.
3) Have Student A return and choose an activity for the group to do together.
4) The group then does the activity with their chosen emotion.
5) Student A then guesses the emotion.
6) Repeat with Student B leaving the room.

Variation:

- The class can choose the activity and the emotion. The student who leaves can guess both.

Reflections:

- What did you do to show emotion?
- What did you do to detect emotion?

SECTION 8: DIALOGUE

✓ Utilizes reasoning skills

✓ Encourages understanding of multiple perspectives

✓ Examines ideas, assumptions, and beliefs

✓ Collectively seeks truth

APPLES TO APPLES DEBATES

⭐ ⭐ ⭐ ⭐ ⭐

About:	A game of persuasion, creative thinking, and lots of laughter
Type of Game:	Dialogue
SEL Standard:	Relationship Skills / Responsible Decision Making
Time:	20 – 30 mins

Supplies:

- Two games of Apples to Apples Junior

Instructions:

1) Divide the class into 5 groups.

2) Have the dealer distribute 7 red cards to each player.

3) The dealer displays a green card.

4) Each player chooses the best red card that matches the green card and gives it to the dealer.

5) The dealer initially ranks the cards from worst to best match, placing the cards in front of them from left to right.

6) Starting with the cards on the left, the dealer asks who submitted that card and why the player thought it was the best match.

7) Based on the player's arguments, the dealer changes their rankings.

8) The student with the highest ranking gets a point for that round.

9) Rotate the dealer until everyone gets a chance at being a judge.

10) Replenish each player with 7 total cards.

11) Give the dealer a new set of 7 cards.

12) Place the used cards in a separate pile.

Reflections:

- What was your most creative argument for matching a red card with a green card?
- What was the most interesting match you heard from another student?

SILLY DEBATE

★ ★ ★ ★ ★

About: Great for practicing argumentation with engaging topics
Type of Game: Dialogue
SEL Standard: Relationship Skills / Responsible Decision Making
Time: 20 – 30 mins

Instructions:

1) This can be done in pairs, small groups, a fishbowl, or a whole class discussion.

2) Introduce the question, "Is water wet?" Explain that for this debate, only one person speaks at a time. For small and large groups, you can use a talking piece and pass it to anyone who hasn't spoken before letting someone speak twice.

3) After 5-10 minutes, introduce the second topic, "Is a hotdog a sandwich?"

4) You have the option to ask students to paraphrase what they heard before they speak.

5) Other topics include
   a. "Is cereal a soup?"
   b. "Is a thumb a finger?"
   c. "If you clean out a vacuum cleaner, are *you* a vacuum cleaner?"

Variation:

- Have students debate preferences such as mountains or oceans, cats or dogs, night or day.

Reflections:

- Were you able to communicate your perspective?
- Did you understand the arguments of anyone who disagreed with you?

WHERE DO YOU STAND?

★ ★ ★ ★ ☆

About: A chance to show and share what we think
Type of Game: Dialogue
SEL Standard: Relationship Skills / Responsible Decision Making
Time: 10 – 20 mins

Instructions:

1) Explain that you will read some statements that students might agree or disagree with.
2) If they strongly agree, they will lean towards the left side of their seat.
3) If they strongly disagree, they will lean towards the right side of their seat.
4) Tell students to modify the depth of their lean based on how strongly they agree or disagree with the statement.
5) Ask students to share the reason for the depth of their leaning.
6) Welcome other students to modify their lean based on the merits and arguments of what other students share.
7) When the energy dies down, introduce a new topic.

Sample Statements:

- Playing a game is fun only when you win.
- Decisions that people make quickly are always wrong.
- Luck has nothing to do with success.
- It's ok to lie.
- Exams are the best way to motivate students.
- Life is easier for children now than fifty years ago.
- People behave differently when they wear different styles of clothing.
- Never, never give up.
- Technology has made the world a better place to live.
- Watching television is bad for children.

Reflections:
- What did you notice about where you stood?
- Were there times you changed your mind after hearing others share their points of view?
- Which arguments were more effective and why?

FISHBOWL

About: Great conversations happen when everyone is watching
Type of Game: Dialogue
SEL Standard: Relationship Skills / Responsible Decision Making
Time: 10 – 20 mins

Instructions:

1) Clear a small circle for 5-6 students in the middle of the classroom which we will call "the fishbowl."
2) Ask for volunteers to be a focus group on a controversial subject.
3) Introduce the topic and let the students control the direction and content of the discussion.

Reflections:

- Which points did you agree with or disagree with?
- Was it easy or hard to listen/or be in the fishbowl?

Variations:

- Have an empty extra seat in the circle for someone on the outside to join the conversation for a moment if they have a burning question or want to make a point.
- Have the students watching the fishbowl rate the arguments they heard on a scale of 1-10.

Teacher Notes:

- This is a great exercise before students write about a topic.
- It's an option to introduce readings and/or videos from multiple perspectives beforehand.

SECTION 9:
ACADEMIC REVIEW

✓ Incorporates multiple learning styles

✓ Integrates knowledge through games

✓ Facilitates peer support

✓ Strengthens communal intellectual rigor

KABOOM

⭐ ⭐ ⭐ ⭐ ⭐

About:	Group bonding through group decisions
Type of Game:	Academic Review
SEL Standard:	Social Awareness / Relationship Skills
Time:	10 – 15 mins

Supplies:

- Computer with internet access for each student

Instructions:

1) Go to *www.KaBoom.org* and set up a multiple-choice quiz for your class.
2) Divide students into groups of four.
3) Explain to groups that they must come to a consensus on the answers. Remind them that the quicker they submit the answer, the more points they receive.
4) Have groups decide on one student who will login and input answers.
5) Ask students to come up with a group name.
6) Start the quiz.

Reflections:

- How did the time pressure affect group decision making?
- What are the decisions you must make in your everyday life that are influenced by time?

GUESS WHO

★ ★ ★ ★ ☆

About: The right question always leads to the right answer
Type of Game: Academic Review
SEL Standard: Social Awareness / Relationship Skills
Time: 5 – 10 mins

Supplies:

- A pack of index cards

Instructions:

1) On a pack of index cards, write a variety of academic vocabulary, content, and concepts.
2) Stack these cards face down in a pile.
3) Ask one student to come to the front of the class and choose a card.
4) Have the student hold the card in front of him or her so that only the class can see the content of the card.
5) The students get to ask the class seven yes or no questions to figure out the content of the card.
6) The class can only respond yes or no.

Variations:

- Have one student leave the class and have the rest of the students choose academic content you want them to review. The student returns to the class and gets to ask yes or no questions to figure out what the students chose for them.
- Give everyone a card and have them ask a yes or no question with another student. After students give each other answers, they thank each other and find a new student to ask a yes or no question until they figure out the content of the card.

Reflections:

- What strategy did you use for creating questions?
- Why are clarifying questions important in life?

FLASH CARD FINISH

★ ★ ★ ☆ ☆

About: Questions that help you remember
Type of Game: Academic Review
SEL Standard: Social Awareness / Relationship Skills
Time: 25 - 30 mins

Supplies:
- Markers
- (200) 3x5 inch Index Cards

Instructions:
1) Divide the class into groups of four.
2) Give each group 10 index cards.
3) Give each group five minutes to create 10 review questions on one side of an index card.
4) Have the students write the answers on the other side.
5) If there is extra time, have the group decorate the cards.
6) Have the group stack their cards and transfer them clockwise to the next group.
7) Give 5 minutes for each group collectively to answer the questions on the new set of index cards.
8) Repeat until each group reads every set of questions.

Variation:
- Make the activity competitive by having each group tally how many questions they answered correctly.

Reflections:
- Did writing questions for other students help you review what you learned?
- What unique questions did you create?

SECTION 10: ENDINGS

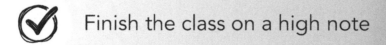 Finish the class on a high note

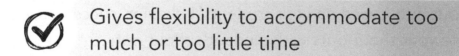 Gives flexibility to accommodate too much or too little time

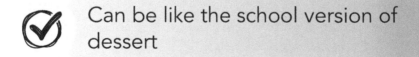 Can be like the school version of dessert

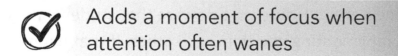 Adds a moment of focus when attention often wanes

SHOUT OUTS

About: Being heard and seen
Type of Game: Endings
SEL Standard: Social Awareness / Relationship Skills
Time: 5 mins or less

Instructions:

1) Ask students to give a positive shout-out to someone in the class for:
   a. Support
   b. Insight
   c. Appreciation
   d. Kindness
   e. Resilience

Variations:

- Give shout-outs based on your students' behavior, successes, etc.
- Alternate your shout-outs with student's shout-outs.
- Ask students to give themselves self appreciation also.

Teacher Note:

- Sometimes students will shout-out something you did. This can be useful feedback and feels great. However, be aware that students might be more comfortable complimenting you than each other. If that happens, consider asking the students to focus on shout-outs only to each other.

RIDDLES, BRAIN TEASERS, AND DETECTIVE STORIES

About: Stretching the mind one last time
Type of Game: Endings
SEL Standard: Social Awareness / Relationship Skills
Time: 5 mins or less

Instructions:

1) Share your favorite riddle, brain teaser, or detective stories.
2) Give time for students to try to guess the answer.
3) If necessary, give stronger and stronger hints until they figure it out.

Resources:

- "Riddles and Trick Questions for Kids and Family" by Playspace, CreateSpace Independent Publishing Platform (March 14, 2016).
- "The Awesome Book of One-Minute Mysteries and Brain Teasers" by Sandy Silverthorne and John Warner, Harvest House Publishers (February 1, 2013).
- "Difficult Riddles for Smart Kids" by M. Prefontaine, CreateSpace Independent Publishing Platform (May 17, 2017).

LIKED, LEARNED, AND/OR LOOKING FORWARD TO

About: Precious feedback and opportunity for review
Type of Game: Endings
SEL Standard: Social Awareness / Relationship Skills
Time: 5 mins or less

Instructions:

1) Ask students to share what they liked, learned, and/or are looking forward to. This might include:
   a. What they enjoyed about the lesson.
   b. New knowledge or understanding.
   c. The way the lesson was taught.
   d. Something they appreciate or learned about someone else.
   e. Something they appreciated or learned about themselves.
   f. Anything that they are excited about, at any point in the future.

Variation:

- Ask students to show their level of satisfaction about the class by how low or high they place their hand in the air.

Teacher Notes:

- It can be useful if you model this reflective activity first.
- Sometimes students will ask to share something they didn't like. Welcome any feedback, as it can be crucial for future planning or a constructive private conversation.
- If time permits, give an opportunity for every student to answer this prompt.

ABOUT THE AUTHOR

David Paris is an educational consultant with *Dance Communication Educators* and is Director of Social Emotional Learning at Middle School 88 in Brooklyn. He has 30 years of experience teaching in NYC public schools and is a *Teach for America* alumni. He is the author of four adolescent fiction books and founder of the *Life Goals in the Classroom* curriculum. He is a group facilitator of *Non-Violent Communication* (NYCNVC.ORG) and is a trainer with *Alternative to Violence Program* (AVPUSA.Org). In his spare time, David teaches and performs acrobatics and dance. David is a seven-time acrobatic dance champion, co-director of Paradizo Dance, and was a finalist on America's Got Talent.

For more information on his projects, go to
www.DavidParisBooks.com
www.Paradizodance.com
www.SELLifeSkills.com

Made in United States
North Haven, CT
16 April 2023